Introduc

Yate

Hi

First, let me thank you for purchasing this book. It was orginally written in 1988. And amazingly it is just as true today as it was then. I first met Ross in early 1990 and after reading this book I called him. I explained to him that I understood what he was doing with neurolinguistic programming and that it was absolutely brilliant, unique and outrageously funny. A business relationship blossomed from that meeting that continues today.

Now let's imagine Ross back then, he had just made his initial breakthroughs with women. Up until then, he had experienced years of frustration in understanding and dealing with women. He then discovered how to use the power of his own mind to view things differently. Ross set about to give other men that power also, in a simple manner that they could APPLY immediately.

He did not bother to explain the technology behind this book or even to tell you that there was a very powerful technology at work. He just wrote, as he puts it on the cover, **"A Down And Dirty Guide To Dating And Seduction For The Man Who's Fed Up With Being Mr. Nice Guy."** Now, as you read the nitroglycerin that follows, you may think that Ross had a bad attitude toward women. You might think you might think that only because you recognized the frustration that had built up and mistook it for something else. Remember this book was written in 1988, a tremondous amount of change has taken place. Ross has even suggested that we take the book off the market as it does not reflect him today. My answer is, "SO WHAT". Picture taking the Bible off the market today because it doesn't reflect the world today, or Richard Bandler taking <u>"Frogs into Princes"</u> off the market. The book is still the best applied seduction technology available today in concise written form to get a person jump started into a new world.

Maybe you have felt compelled at some point in your life to read between the lines, as I did when I first read this book. For example, in Chapter 10, Slashing Comebacks for Sleazoid Sluts, Ross is really saying you must preserve you self esteem at all cost. As you see yourself approaching a woman in an appropriate manner and saying, "Excuse me, can I ask you a question"; what do you do when she is RUDE. If you walk away and do not respond, YOU ARE AGREEING WITH WHATEVER HER RUDE DEROGATORY COMMENTS WERE TOWARD YOU. You must RESPOND to let her know that she is being rude, not you doing anything inappropriate. Ross does this is a comical way that is very effective.

This book has become the tip of the seduction iceberg, or the foundation of what NOW is copyrighted and trademarked by Ross as "Speed Seduction". Ross continues to push the envelope of seduction using neurolinguistic programming, Erickson hypnosis, and psychic power. He has developed basic and advanced home study courses in video and audio, 3-day seminars on seduction and 7-day seminars on Speed Life.

Returning to the example above, you could respond, "Thank you for letting me know what kind person you really are. I could have spent a lot of time and money to find this out. So thank you again and I just want to let you know your rudeness doesn't affect me. You are the one who has to live with yourself for the rest of your like."

So, enjoy reading, between the lines, and more. We will see you at the TOP if you are willing to suspend your beliefs for a short time and just do what Ross says. Remember, it's your brain and you have to go first.

DISCLAIMER

Neither the author nor the publisher assumes any responsibility for the use or misuse of information contained in this book. The reader is warned that the use of some or all of the techniques in this book may result in legal consequences, civil and/or criminal. USE OF THIS BOOK IS DONE AT YOUR OWN RISK.

"He who will not take the hint, must take the consequences." — — Glenn v. Covey 282 PA 367 (1854)

ISBN 0-963037900
©1992 Jeffries Publishing

Author's Note

If you have a favorite pick-up line, seductive technique or story, that you would like to send me, send to:

Ross Jeffries
6245 Bristol Parkway, Suite 275
Culver City CA 90230

TABLE OF CONTENTS

INTRODUCTION 1

PART ONE: HOW TO HAVE POWER AND CONFIDENCE WITH WOMEN 5

CHAPTER ONE: THE ONE ATTITUDE THAT IS THE KEY TO HAVING IRRESISTIBLE APPEAL TO WOMEN AND GETTING LAID WITH THE WOMEN OF YOUR DREAMS 5

CHAPTER TWO: HOW TO INSTALL THE SUPER-GET LAID ATTITUDES IN YOURSELF SO YOU USE THEM AUTOMATICALLY 9

CHAPTER THREE: BELIEVE IT OR NOT, HOW TO HAVE EVEN MORE CONFIDENCE WITH WOMEN ..11

CHAPTER FOUR: STILL MORE CONFIDENCE AND POWER WITH WOMEN! 13

CHAPTER FIVE: YET MORE CONFIDENCE AND POWER WITH WOMEN 15

PART TWO: HOW TO MEET WOMEN, ANYTIME, ANYWHERE 16

CHAPTER SIX: HOW TO FAKE LIKE YOU ARE WARM AND FRIENDLY 17

CHAPTER SEVEN: GETTING HER ATTENTION - THE KEY TO PICK UPS WHEREVER YOU ARE 21

CHAPTER EIGHT: HOW TO MAKE A WOMAN YOU'VE JUST MET FEEL LIKE SHE'S MET THE MAN OF HER DREAMS 23

CHAPTER NINE: SOME GREAT METHODS AND GREAT PLACES TO PICK UP MORE WOMEN THAN YOU AND A FRIEND COULD POSSIBLY HOPE TO HANDLE INCLUDING THE ONLY TWO PICK-UP LINES IN THE WORLD THAT WORK SO WELL THAT THEY CAN GET YOU LAID AUTOMATICALLY 25

CHAPTER TEN: SLASHING COMEBACKS FOR SLEAZOID SLUTS! 37

CHAPTER ELEVEN: HOW TO USE THE PERSONALS TO GET HUNDREDS AND HUNDREDS OF WOMEN TO DATE! 39

CHAPTER TWELVE: BIRDOGGING: How To Get A Girl When She's With Another Guy (Or When You're With Another Girl) 43

CHAPTER THIRTEEN: GETTING THE DATE 45

CHAPTER FOURTEEN: GETTING THE PHONE NUMBER ROUTE 47

CHAPTER FIFTEEN: MAKING THE DATE ON THE SPOT 51

CHAPTER SIXTEEN: HOW TO HANDLE BITCHES WHO TRY TO CANCEL DATES 53

PART THREE: HOW TO GET THE WOMEN YOU DATE INTO BED 57

CHAPTER SEVENTEEN: DECIDING YOUR APPROACH. 57

CHAPTER EIGHTEEN: HOW TO USE HYPNOSIS TO GET YOUR DATE INTO THE SACK 59

CHAPTER NINETEEN: HOW TO TOTALLY BREAK A WOMAN'S RESISTANCE TO SLEEPING WITH YOU 71

CHAPTER TWENTY: A FINAL WORD 75

APPENDIX ONE: THE ULTIMATE RULES AND ATTITUDES FOR SUCCESS WITH WOMEN 77

APPENDIX TWO: REPRESENTATIONAL SYSTEMS ..79

APPENDIX THREE: INDUCING TRANCE STATES IN YOUR DATE USING THE STORY TELLING METHOD 80

APPENDIX FOUR: THE RIGHT WAY TO USE VISUALIZATION TO BUILD IRRESISTIBLE CONFIDENCE 81

APPENDIX FIVE: ANCHORING TO BUILD CONFIDENCE 82

APPENDIX SIX: HOW TO SWIFTLY DETECT AND ELIMINATE WOMEN WHO ARE WACKOS, LOW-LIFES, CRAZIES AND SCUM 83

INTRODUCTION

UNFAIR SEDUCTIONS IN AN UNFAIR WORLD

Many people who read the rough draft of this book were upset by parts of it. Invariably, I'd hear the same complaint. "These tactics you're teaching probably work really well. We thought the parts on power and confidence and on meeting women were great. But some of the actual seduction techniques are down right dishonest and unfair. They really don't give the woman any choice. Why don't you just leave them out of the book? Then no one could possibly have any objections." OK. Let's get the "unfair" charge out of the way. Yes, some, and I mean SOME of the seduction tactics in this book could easily be classified as "unfair." And, truth to tell, I had some serious moral reservations about putting them in the book. However, "unfair" and "fair" are relative terms. If you and I are in a boxing match, and we are both fighting by the rules, then it is totally unfair for me to kick you in the nuts and poke you in the eyes. You are fighting by the rules, and so should I.

But, if YOU start fighting dirty, I will feel under no moral obligation whatsoever to continue to stand there like a fool and take it. I'm going to toss out all the rules and fight to win, no matter what it takes.

Unfortunately, when you deal with women, you may often find yourself in that type of situation. They expect you to play by the rules, but they feel perfectly free to do whatever THEY want. For example, lots of women are more than happy to spend your money and time, and generally lead you on, letting you think you have a reward (sexual) coming. They talk about sex on the date, touch you a lot, and ACT very seductive. Then when you make a pass, they freak out and scream about what animals men are, how we're only after one thing. Or they let you have it with that famous line "I'm just not attracted to you." Maybe you find out that she was just using you as a social "spare tire" because her boyfriend was out of town for a few weeks and she didn't want to sit at home alone and look at the four walls.

Of course, if you really want to be a "gentleman" you may not find any of this out until the third or fourth date. You don't want to behave like an animal and make a pass on the first date, do you? So you hold off awhile, and then the slap in the face hurts even more.

Now, any chick who pulls this off DESERVES to be on the receiving end of the most unfair tactics you can use. You are under no moral obligation to be her victim, and you are a fool if you permit it.

So, by all means, play fair with a woman until she shows you that she is playing unfair with you. As soon as she starts to pull shit, then either walk away completely or let her have it with everything you have in your arsenal.

And while we're on the subject of fair, is it "fair" that the good-looking and rich guys should get all the beautiful women while you and I have to settle for the dogs? Are you any less deserving of complete sexual satisfaction than some pretty boy who was blessed by genetics and Daddy's bank account? Why should you just meekly roll over, and accept a situation that **SUCKS,** good buddy, when you can be getting your share, and then some!

Something else to consider: When it comes to sex, women have a **massive power advantage.** It's relatively easy for even a fat, ugly troll to obtain sexual satisfaction. All she has to do is go to any bar or club, act even mildly flirtatious, and be willing to put out. She's sure to get laid, if not by the best looking guy, then at least by someone.

It's much harder for even a decent looking guy to get satisfaction, sexually. FOR GUYS, GETTING LAID IS A CHORE. FOR WOMEN, GETTING LAID IS A CHOICE. Never forget this difference in the balance of power between the sexes. The tricks and tactics you'll learn in this book will make you one of those rare guys who is on the choice side of that power equation.

OK. While we are here I better make something clear. I do NOT believe that sex is the be all and end all of relating to women. Nor do I believe that it is always necessary or even DESIRABLE to use the tactics outlined in this book, (whether fair or unfair) to get a woman to sleep with you. It is certainly possible that the particular woman you fancy may be smart enough and have enough good sense to want you just as you are, without any games or bullshit on her part. She may also be sane and psychologically healthy enough to express that desire naturally, without any hang-ups or guilt games. You might even find — gasp — that the friendship and intimacy you share with a lady are more important to you than sex. When you find a lady like this, cherish her as the rare treasure she is. Hang on tight, and don't let go!

Unfortunately, based on my own experience, and the experience of hundreds of men I've interviewed, most women do not fit into this category. I wish they did - the REALITY is that they do NOT! The reality is that you, as a man, are going to be sexually attracted to many, many women, very few of whom are going to naturally desire you, and who you can also respect, love and admire.

Many of these women are going to be hung-up sexually, depressed, suffer from low self-esteem, eating disorders, alcoholism, etc. Heck, I even briefly dated a woman who turned out to be bulimic, alcoholic, and was also secretly a hooker! Top that for a dating disaster story!

Now, you may decide, the heck with it. If you can't at least like and respect a lady, and if you have to resort to tactics you learned in a book, then it just isn't worth it, and you will skip dealing with such loser females altogether. I certainly can respect that choice; it's the choice I eventually made myself. But only YOU can make that choice. Even if you do, this book will still be of great value to you, because you will learn fantastic techniques for improving your confidence, meeting and picking up women anywhere, any time, and how to quickly recognize and swiftly eliminate all the nutty-losers BEFORE they get to empty your wallet, bend your brain, and kick your heart in. You'll be able to get rid of the dirt, so you can enjoy the diamonds.

A FEW MORE WORDS BEFORE WE GET ON WITH THIS BOOK

There's one big mistake that all the so called "Pick-up Chicks" books seem to make. That is, THEY DON'T TELL YOU HOW TO HAVE THE CONFIDENCE AND POWER TO ACTUALLY GO OUT AND USE ALL THEIR GREAT "SEDUCTION" SUGGESTIONS.

This is a CRITICAL mistake. Great advice does you no good at all if you can't actually go out and APPLY it. All it really does is make you feel worse, because now you know what to do but you STILL can't do it. At least when you were ignorant you had an excuse.

This book will NOT make that mistake; in fact the whole first section is dedicated to showing you how to have the confidence and power to be able to easily use and apply the tactics in the other two sections of the book. We'll also show you how to use your own creativity so you can develop your own seduction tactics that perfectly fit your unique personality and circumstances.

Not bad for one little book, huh?

A FINAL WORD

Throughout this book, I will be laying down certain ideas that you would do well to memorize and use. I suggest you get some 3 x 5 index cards to write these ideas down so you can go over them as you need to. There will also be exercises to do. It is ESSENTIAL that you DO THE EXERCISES. Just reading them will get you nowhere.

Enough chit chat. Let's go to battle men.

PART ONE:

HOW TO HAVE POWER AND CONFIDENCE WITH WOMEN

CHAPTER ONE:

THE ONE ATTITUDE THAT IS THE KEY TO HAVING IRRESISTIBLE APPEAL TO WOMEN AND GETTING LAID WITH THE WOMEN OF YOUR DREAMS

Once, one of my super-scoring buddies invited me to go to a party with him. Not having much of a social life anyway, I accepted the invitation, and besides, this guy REALLY knew how to get laid. I sort of looked at myself as being one of those small sucker fish that attach themselves underneath a shark's mouth and live off the bits the shark spits out.

Anyway, we were wandering around this huge apartment complex, looking for the party. We were walking down a hallway when we passed an open door, and there was a party going on, but it was definitely NOT the party we had been invited too. This was a formal affair; everyone was very well dressed, and my buddy and I were both wearing jeans and scruffy tennis shoes.

Through the doorway I saw a stunning blonde in a low cut dress, surrounded by guys trying to hit on her. My buddy saw her too, looked at me, and went right into action. I saw him walk in the door, cut through the crowd of guys, say something to her that I couldn't hear, and hand her a card and a pen. She wrote something down, and out came my buddy, smiling ear to ear. He had gotten her phone number!

I asked him what he said, and he told me, "I just walked in there, looked at her, and said, Excuse me. I saw you through the doorway, and unlike these gentlemen here, I don't have time for small talk. I'd like to take you out. Can I have your home phone number?'"

Now, it's not always necessary to be that direct. But it is necessary to grasp and use the attitude my buddy had, the super-attitude which will get you laid more than any line, trick, good looks, fancy car or fortune. The attitude is:

I MAKE NO EXCUSES FOR MY DESIRES AS A MAN. I MAKE NO EXCUSES FOR MYSELF. I MOVE THROUGH THE WORLD WITHOUT APOLOGY

Do you really want to get laid with all the women you could ever possibly want? Then STOP MAKING EXCUSES FOR YOURSELF! Don't make excuses for wanting to look at a beautiful woman. If you're caught looking, and she asks what you're doing, tell her!! Tell her you're enjoying studying just what a perfectly beautiful body she has, and to heck with her if she's too uptight to appreciate a real man who doesn't apologize for knowing what he wants!

Stop making excuses for wanting to meet a woman! Stop making excuses for wanting to ask a woman out, and most of all stop making excuses for wanting to FUCK the living shit out of a woman you want! This kind of direct, powerful, go-for-it-attitude is an incredible turn on for women that can't be beaten!

Listen! It isn't even the words you use that convey this attitude! It's your tone of voice, your facial expressions, your posture, the speed at which you speak, everything non-verbal about you will show this attitude **far** more than words.

This doesn't mean you have to be arrogant, or lack a sense of humor. You can be warm and friendly at the same time you are being direct and **powerful**. The key is finding the balance. Once you do you will not be able to keep women **away from you**.

Now, it's **easy to talk and tell you that you should** have this attitude, but that won't help you to actually get it. That's why the next couple of chapters are so important. They will show you how to install this attitude in yourself so that you **automatically** find yourself living by it in your approach to women. You won't even have to try or to "think about it." It will just happen.

Here's the other attitude/belief you'll want to master if you really want to be a success at scoring with women like a madman.

I DON'T GET RATTLED BY SETBACKS BECAUSE I LEARN FROM MY MISTAKES.

I remember watching a TV show where the host was interviewing a movie star/karate champ who shall go nameless. The host asked him what the secret of his success was, and the karate guy looked at him in that wooden way of his and said:

"When I first started out competing in Karate Tournaments, I wasn't that good. I got beat a lot, but I always learned from my mistakes. Instead of crying over my losing, I just studied what I would have to do differently the next time, and whenever I met the same guy again or a different guy in the same situation, I ALWAYS creamed 'em."

Look — unless you are unusually lucky, chances are you are going to make a few mistakes as you practice the ideas in this book. And, as great as these tricks are, they won't work every single time.

Unless you know how to learn from your mistakes and accept and occasional loss, you will get nowhere. The most successful guys I know at scoring all have two great strengths: They have the first power attitude we've just looked at, and they also know how to accept getting rejected without it bothering them and they learn from their mistakes.

OK. As I promised, let's get on to the next couple of chapters which will show you how to actually live these attitudes instead of just **reading** about them.

CHAPTER TWO

HOW TO INSTALL THE SUPER GET LAID ATTITUDES IN YOURSELF SO YOU USE THEM AUTOMATICALLY

There is one small point you have to get before you can use this exercise. Take a minute to imagine yourself riding in a roller coaster. See yourself sitting in the front car, riding up and down.

Now, make another picture of a roller coaster, but this time, do NOT see yourself in the picture. See it as if you were actually looking out of your own eyes, sitting in the roller coaster. Ride for a few moments.

Now, which one of those felt more real in your body? I'll bet anything it was the second kind. An image or goal only appears real to your mind if it comes in the second form, as if you were seeing it through your own eyes.

THE FAILURE TO UNDERSTAND THIS SIMPLE DIFFERENCE BETWEEN THE TWO KINDS OF MENTAL PICTURES PEOPLE MAKE IS THE SINGLE BIGGEST REASON WHY MOST PEOPLE NEVER REACH THEIR GOALS.

You could imagine yourself acting confident and powerful until you are blue in the face, but unless you give your mind some cues as to when it is going to tap into those pictures you will get NOWHERE. You will never tap into all those great resources you've been imagining.

For ease we are going to call the first kind of picture, where you do see yourself, picture type 1, and the second kind of picture where you do not see yourself, picture type 2.

OK. Now that we have made that clear, let's get on to the exercise.

STEP ONE: Recall a time in your past when you felt confident and powerful. A time where you fully felt the way you'd like to feel around women. This can be anywhere and about anything — a great golf shot you made, or an "A" book report you did in school.

STEP TWO: Close your eyes, and see yourself in the first kind of picture, going through that experience again.

STEP THREE: Now, step into the picture, and see the events as if you were actually looking out from your own eyes. See what you saw, hear what you heard, and feel how good it felt in your body. When those feelings of confidence and power reach their peak in your body, reach over with your right hand, and give your left wrist a squeeze. Run through this twice more, giving the same squeeze in the same place. This will train your mind to recall those feelings of power and confidence whenever you squeeze your wrist the way you are doing now.

STEP FOUR: Think of a situation or circumstance where you would like to be more powerful with women or more poised or whatever it is you'd like.

STEP FIVE: Picture it the second way, as if it were going on and you were seeing it through your own eyes.

STEP SIX: As you do so, reach over with your right hand and squeeze your left wrist, triggering your confidence anchor. This will train your mind to automatically call up the feelings of confidence and power when you are in a situation like the one you are seeing through your own eyes. You won't even have to think about doing it, which is the advantage. (And that's why anchoring works where "positive thinking" won't, because often by the time you get yourself thinking positively, it's already too late.)

Now, once you've done this, I want you to do it again, but this time I want you to pick different circumstances where you'd like to use your "power attitude" that we talked about in the first chapter. Make one a situation where you see a beautiful woman you'd like to talk to. Another could be making a pass at a woman back at your place. Go through the situation with the first kind of picture, seeing yourself in the picture. Then step into the picture, and go through it, feeling what it would feel like, looking through your own eyes. Do the same thing for the second "learning from your mistakes" attitude. See yourself making a mistake, feeling ok about it, and learning whatever lesson you need so you can do it differently next time. Then step into the picture and see it through your own eyes.

CHAPTER THREE

BELIEVE IT OR NOT, HOW TO HAVE EVEN MORE CONFIDENCE WITH WOMEN

A great deal of success and power with women has nothing to do with how you act and feel about them, but a lot to do with how you act and feel about yourself. What we're really talking about here is SELF-RESPECT.

Plenty of men who wouldn't take a bit of crap from another guy turn into down right spineless wimps when it comes to women. Whether they are reliving old dramas with a mommy they couldn't please as children, or are scared for some other reason, they put the woman first.

Other guys have a slightly different problem. They may not take any crap from a woman, but getting laid is SO damn important to them that they lose sight of other priorities. In a sense it loses all the fun aspects, and gets to be a compulsion.

Guys like this may win the battles, but they are definitely losing the war. Women may be nice additions to your life, and if you find the right one, you might even chose to make her part of the center of yours. But a life spent doing nothing but chasing women is a pretty stupid one.

If that is your problem, then pull yourself up short for a minute, and ask yourself if you might be missing some of the other pleasures life has to offer. You might be shocked to learn that a quiet evening at home with a good book can actually be more stimulating than a boring date with a huge breasted bimbo with a room temperature I.Q.

So here's a hint for increasing your confidence with women: STOP NEEDING THEM SO MUCH! And a good way to do that is going out and finding a hobby that you can really enjoy. Something that gets you AWAY from women.

Not only will this increase your confidence as you are on the prowl, it provides a great escape for when that special lady you are with puts a bit of stress and strain on your brain, as they so often will.

Personally, I prefer Big Mouth Bass Fishing. Most women hate even the thought of some icky, slimy fish flopping all over them, and wouldn't even consider asking to go along with you. And besides, I enjoy catching something with a big mouth, and being able to instantly throw it away if I feel like it. Women are not so easy.

CHAPTER FOUR

STILL MORE CONFIDENCE AND POWER WITH WOMEN!

Here is a magic word that will bring you loads of success with women, and get you laid like crazy. It works with all women, but the more beautiful the woman, the better it works. The word is: NO!

That's right. No! The same word that will keep a puppy from wetting the carpet will also keep a woman from shitting on you!

You must say no to a woman once in a while, when it is over an issue of importance, and when you mean it.

No matter how gorgeous, or great in the sack or how otherwise wonderful she may be (and who else but such a goddess could possibly begin to deserve to be in YOUR company?) you must be willing to walk away from her if you can't deal with her from a position of self-respect.

And self-respect, my friend, is mostly a matter of what you say no to. It's a boundary set by what is not permitted, tolerated or allowed. And while it may be negative from this semantic sense, in reality it is the most power and positive force you have going for you. When a woman senses it in you, she knows she's found something she's instinctively wanted since she realized she's female: A MAN SHE COULD NEVER HOPE TO CONTROL.

I know this isn't easy. It hurts, really hurts to have to walk away from someone you really dig because she isn't treating you right. But love can often be like a street fight, and remember the street fighter's number one rule: Ignore the pain and carry out your offensive with everything you've got. If you can pull this off, you will walk with a confidence and power that women of all ages will be able to sense. And more importantly, you'll like the guy who lives inside your skin.

CHAPTER FIVE

YET MORE CONFIDENCE AND POWER WITH WOMEN

George S. Patton Jr., the hell-for-leather General of World War II fame was once asked what he thought of his rival, the British Field Marshall Montgomery. Patton replied, "He's the best General the British have. But he's more interested in not losing than he is in winning. Unfortunately for many men, that's their attitude toward women. They walk on egg-shells, cautious as can be, hoping against hope that they don't make a mistake.

If you want to have DYNAMIC power with women, begin to focus on what you want, and what you are going to do, not on what you might lose or what's going to happen to you if you don't win. Of course, give the risks a glance. But don't focus on them.

Focus on what you desire. What will it be like when you're with that woman you want? What will you see? What will you hear? What will you feel in your body?

These are the kinds of questions that will get you excited about and aimed at winning, instead of cringing at losing. Even if you know you have some competition you'll be able to give it you're best shot, because your major focus will be on your outcome.

In short: GLANCE AT WHAT YOU MIGHT HAVE TO LOSE, BUT FOCUS ON WHAT YOU WANT TO WIN.

PART TWO

HOW TO MEET WOMEN, ANYTIME, ANYWHERE

(In which we look at the four steps to any pick-up)

1. Getting Attention

2. Making your introduction

3. Creating rapport

4. Making your pitch

CHAPTER SIX

HOW TO FAKE LIKE YOU ARE WARM AND FRIENDLY

When I was in college, and struggling just to get a date, let alone get laid right and left, I knew one guy who ALWAYS had great looking women around him. He seemed to know practically every girl on campus, and they'd always come up to him and give him hugs and kisses. No, he was not a coke dealer or a pimp. Of all things, he was an evangelist.

Now, I'm certainly not advocating Jesus Freakery as the way to get your weenie wet. But you might take a few lessons from this guy, Chris. I'd watch him go to work on women who were absolute strangers and within a few minutes, they'd be laughing and punching him playfully, sometimes giving him hugs. If it weren't for the Lord, Chris would have been the big stud on campus.

And what was his secret, a secret I hope YOU use to launch you on the way to getting laid like a bandit? His affinity and warmth made women feel ADORED. He didn't come on all hot and heavy, like a hungry wolf on the prowl. He came on with all the friendliness and fun at his disposal — as if these strange women were long lost friends that he dearly loved.

And they bought it! Even the chickiest woman, who is very uptight about being a sex object, wants to feel loved and special. And just by the warmth in the tone of his voice and his smile he made these girls feel as if they WERE long lost friends.

Look at it this way: Even the nastiest person finds it hard to react fearfully or angrily to someone who makes them feel loved and appreciated.

I suggest you make this AS IF principle part of your bag of tricks. The next time you approach a woman who is making you burst out of your pants with lust, try putting aside the lust and turning on the warmth.

Conveying warmth and affinity isn't so tough — just think of how you look and sound when you see a niece or nephew, or even a pet that delights you. No, I am not suggesting baby talk as a way of scoring babes. I'm trying to give you an example of where it's natural for you to behave the way I'd like you to try behaving with women.

The important principle to apply here is that THE MEANING OF YOUR COMMUNICATION IS THE RESPONSE IT GETS. If you use a tone of voice or a facial expression that makes women fearful or suspicious, then no matter how clever your words are, the message you convey to her is that she should be afraid and suspicious of you.

If voice tone and physiology (and again I don't mean your appearance per se, but rather your posture and facial expressions) are so crucial in how women react to you, then what is the key to producing voice tone and physiology? Your belief and expectation about your outcome.

If you believe you are going to get rejected then you are either going to convey fear, and make her fearful or else you are going to try to beat her to the punch and act so obnoxious that she rejects you right off, so you don't have to wait too long in suspense for your negative prediction to come true. You just want to get it over with quickly so you actually produce the humiliation that you believe you cannot avoid.

By contrast, if you act as if you truly were someone who everyone liked and received warmly, then that warmth is what your tone and physiology will convey, and that's the response you will get, nine times out of ten. I'm not saying you'll get laid with everyone you approach, but seldom will you have a nasty experience either. And any woman who doesn't respond positively to warmth and affinity is seriously sick and should be avoided at all costs anyway.

PRACTICE EXERCISE: OK, I know this one is going to SEEM a little silly, but it's going to help you get laid like CRAZY, so just do it!

Step One: Remember the words to the pledge of allegiance. In case you don't here they are: (You may stand and put your hand over your heart if you so choose):

I pledge allegiance to the flag of the United States of America, and to the Republic for which it stands, one nation, under God, indivisible, with liberty and justice for all.

Step Two: Practice, out loud, saying these words with all the warmth and friendliness you can muster.

Step Three: Practice saying them out loud as if you thought they were the funniest thing in the world and you might crack up laughing at any moment.

OK, so you feel a bit silly practicing (and if someone should catch you they may think you've joined the John Birch Society) and it seems weird. But just remember — IT ISN'T SO MUCH WHAT YOU SAY TO A WOMAN, BUT YOUR TONE OF VOICE WHEN YOU SAY IT!!!!

CHAPTER SEVEN

GETTING HER ATTENTION
THE KEY TO PICK-UPS WHEREVER YOU ARE

I have a brother who's in advertising — more specifically he writes newspaper and magazine ad copy. I once watched him at work, and he sat for about three hours and then wrote one sentence! One sentence!

I asked him why he took so long on one sentence and his answer stuck with me: It's that first sentence that determines whether they even read the rest of the ad!

Look at meeting women like an ad man who's writing copy for a newspaper ad. Maybe one out of a hundred readers is actively looking for the product you are trying to sell, and they will read your whole ad no matter what the headline says.

The rest of the readers could care less. They are busy flipping pages, trying to get to the comics section or the sports page. They will only stop if something grabs their attention.

So it is with the average chick. In a few lucky situations, your looks alone will snag her. But the rest of the time you won't have much chance of selling your product unless you grab her attention and grab it fast. (I know, you want to grab something else, but that comes later. Animal.)

Below are some of the best ways to grab a girls attention. Keep them in mind as you read the next few chapters.

1. Humor

2. Appealing to her curiosity

3. Putting an unusual or unexpected twist on an old, cliche pick-up

4. Role playing

5. Faking like you already know her

6. Appealing to her ego

7. Showing outrageous balls or guts

CHAPTER EIGHT

HOW TO MAKE A WOMAN YOU'VE JUST MET FEEL LIKE SHE'S MET THE MAN OF HER DREAMS

The next step after you've got her attention is to introduce yourself and get her name. I hope you are smart enough to do that without my advice.

Then you've got to create the illusion of rapport. For those of you who don't know what rapport means, the dictionary defines it as: "Accord, affinity, relations marked by harmony."

The techniques you use to create rapport will vary according to the type of pick-up you are using. Of course, we've already gone over the proper way to use your tone of voice.

Here are two other very sneaky and powerful ways to create rapport with a woman. You should use them when you're actually on a date as well as when you first meet a woman. They take some practice to master, but work quite well.

METHOD ONE: MIRRORING

There once was a very powerful and successful hypnotist by the name of Milton Erickson. When you are through with this book you may well want to build a shrine to Erickson, because this man is going to help get you laid more than having a million dollars cash and a body like Scharwtznegger.

Erickson could hypnotize anyone, even the most resistant patient or client. One of the ways he did this was by mirroring the breathing of the person he was hypnotizing.

Now, I'm going to pause for a minute so you can go through your "Bullshit" reaction. But mirroring someone's breathing is a very powerful way to make them unconsciously feel in tune with you. Erickson would watch the rate of his client's breathing and then begin to match it with his own breathing, or with the pace of his speaking. Or he'd tap his chest with his hand in time to the persons breathing, and then begin to gradually slow the tapping. The persons breathing would slow in time to the tapping!

Mirroring works because your unconscious picks up and is aware of things your conscious mind has no knowledge of. To convince yourself that this is so, try this experiment:

1. Get a friend of yours and have them close their eyes. Ask them to keep their eyes closed, and guess what you are doing.

2. Stand in front of them, and begin speaking. As you do so, sway your head from side to side.

3. Ask them what you are doing.

Of course, they will be able to tell you you are moving your head back and forth. Now, ask them how they knew — they'll tell you they could hear the difference in how you sounded.

Now, try it again, but this time ask them to keep their eyes open. Ask if they can hear the difference now, and of course they can't? Actually, they CAN hear the difference, because they still have the same pair of ears - they just aren't CONSCIOUSLY aware of it. But unconsciously, you bet they are!

In the same way, if you mirror a chick's breathing, or her tone of voice, or rate of speaking, or even a particular gesture she uses, on a conscious level she won't notice. If she does notice on a conscious level, then you are being too obvious and she's either going to think you are a weirdo or are making fun of her, and neither of these will score you points.

But if you do it subtly, then all she will know is that for some odd reason she sure seems to feel right down comfortable with you, old buddy, as if she's loved you for years!

Chances are, she'll be so impressed, **she'll** come over to talk to **you**. This line is <u>very</u> flattering, and what really makes it work is the last bit about "working up the courage to meet you." It implies that she's so beautiful that you just had to overcome all that shyness just so you could get a chance to meet her. Women eat this line like candy and it will get you laid by waitresses, salesgirls and the like with startling frequency.

3. The dirty, sneaky, fake like you are in show biz approach. Here in L.A., 99.999% of the better looking waitresses are aspiring actresses, waiting for that big break. Some of these women are so gorgeous they would make you drool in your pants, and they are ripe for someone who they <u>think</u> can help them along in their career. Now, keeping in mind the ecology warning at the beginning of this chapter, let me tell you how I stumbled on to this scam and how it can help you to sleep with the most beautiful women around.

At the time I stumbled on this approach, I had a roommate who worked for a small aerospace research company. They had just moved into a suite of offices that previously had been occupied by a talent agency. Opening a closet one day, they discovered a few hundred pictures of very good looking actresses who were applying for a role in a film.

My roommate brought about a hundred of them home, and as I was going through them, slobbering all over myself, it suddenly occurred to me that:

A. Most of these girls were probably working as waitresses to support themselves.

B. What better way to get favorable attention from some cutie pie waitress than to walk into a bar or restaurant with these and just start going through them.

So, that's what I did. And sure enough, before long, a very gorgeous young food and drink service technician (bureaucratese for waitress) came by to see what I was doing. I told her that my sister ran a company that makes movies for TV (which happens to be the truth, but don't worry if you don't have a sister that does that, you can talk about <u>my</u> sister if you feel guilty) and that she wanted me to go through these pictures and select the ones I thought were the most attractive. Naturally, this sweetie pie was an aspiring future Oscar winner, and asked if she could get a resume to me. I said it would have to be fast, as my sister wanted to know by tomorrow. Of course, she invited me to come back to her place after work to get the picture, and well, we had a few drinks and........

The key to this method is not to make it seem like you are blackmailing her. Tell her you would be happy to submit her picture and resume to the right person. After you have agreed to that, THEN ask her out. The threat of you not doing it if she doesn't accept hasn't been made, and nice guy that you are, you wouldn't even think of <u>implying</u> it. But <u>she</u> might be afraid of losing your good will, and so will accept. Try to get her to go out with you on the spot.

Now, some of you may be wondering, "Well, it sounds great. But what if I don't have a roommate who happens to work for an aerospace research company that happens to be in the same office that used to be used by a talent agency?"

Good question. What you do is put a simple ad in your local paper along these lines:

"Models wanted! All expenses paid, plus $500.00 photo shoot in Tahiti! Send 8 x 10 to: Your Name Productions, Your Address."

That should get you some nice responses.

Street and Supermarket Pickups

One of the toughest places to pick-up women is right on the street, and that's why I love it; it's a real challenge.

Of course, one of the easy ways out is the old "taking a survey" method, but that isn't nearly as much fun as using lines.

The absolute key to street pick-ups is to be very upbeat, happy, warm and friendly. Do NOT come on heavy on the street. Women are naturally (and justly) cautious in the big city.

Here's a great street pick-up for you that will also work in a supermarket. I call it the compliment string.

Pick out your target, then walk alongside her. Find one thing about her you can genuinely compliment, then say:

"I like your hat."

She'll say "Thank you."

Then say, "I like your watch."

She'll say "Thank you."

Then what you do is pause, sort of look at her sideways for a moment, and say with as much charm and good humor as you can:

"Come to think of it, I like everything."

Nine times out of ten that will get a big laugh. If she doesn't laugh, she's a very uptight chick and you'd just get rejected if you straight asked her out anyway.

Once she's laughed you hit her with this:

"My name's _____. By what name are you called, you shining example of genetic perfection?" (I know that sounds corny but it will get a big laugh. Trust me.)

Once she tells you, you say, "You know, I can tell you're woman with fantastic good taste. And you know how I know that?"

She'll ask how.

"Because you laugh at all of my jokes."

She'll laugh again. Then you hit her with another laugh line.

"Do you believe in irrational and self-defeating infatuation at first sight?"

She'll laugh again. If she says yes, then you should jokingly look heavenward and say "Thank you, God. Would you like to get a cup of coffee?" If she says no (to the infatuation question, not your coffee invitation), you say, "Great. Then I'm not being irrational if I ask you to have a cup of coffee (or some frozen yogurt, or whatever is nearby and convenient).

Whatever the response, you want to try to invite her to do something with you, in a public place, right then and there.

If she says she'd like to, but is in a hurry to get somewhere, ask her out for that evening, if it is at all feasible. Say something like "I'd be very flattered if you'd have dinner with me tonight." Be direct, but charming at the same time, and don't back down! Your very directness is part of what makes you appealing, and when you combine it with charm, a smile, and the ability to make her laugh, you are really going to hit her hard. And that bit about being "flattered." Well, for some reason I can't figure, that works <u>very</u> well. Make sure you add that in. It's like you're saying that the nicest compliment about yourself would be to be seen in public with her.

This approach will also work well in a supermarket. It's unique, different, funny, direct, and fun and romantic for you <u>and</u> her.

I discovered another great supermarket pick-up totally by accident. I was suffering through another attack of hayfever during allergy season, so I went to the local Osco drug store to get something for it. As I was walking along I spied an incredible honey wearing very tight jeans and an equally tight T-shirt. As I walked by her, I had to sneeze, but the sneeze wouldn't come out, so I paused right next to her as I struggled to sneeze. I noticed her looking at me, and instantly my magnificently sleazy brain phonied up a scam.

With one finger up to my nose, as if I were about to sneeze, I said to her, "Do me a favor. Pound me really hard on the back."

She said, "Are you sure?"

I said, "Yes."

She gave me a good slap, and I said, "Well, it didn't help the sneeze, but I think I just fell in love. What's your name?"

Then I hit her with the other lines you've already seen. Unfortunately, she was married. Oh well. But I've used the line on other occasions with success. It's a numbers game, good buddy, a numbers game. But you'll find this "sneeze" line works well in just about any public "non-pick-up" setting, such as the beach, parks, etc. Try it, and you'll see it's nothing to sneeze at. Ha ha ha ha ha ha ha. That's what's called an author's right to abuse his readers.

How To Ask A Woman Out When You're Both In Front Of Other People

Once I was in barber shop, getting my hair cut, and an incredibly sexy lady was waiting her turn. She was wearing a skirt that was so short that you could easily see her juicy thighs. Her legs were screaming out to be mine, but what could I do? Although I was busy chatting with her in front of the barber and the other people waiting their turn, I couldn't graciously ask her out right there in front of everyone, could I?

I started reviewing my other options. I could hang around after my haircut, and wait for her to finish, and then hit her as she was coming out the door, but that would be lame, and kind of scary for her.

Well, I did a little mental exercise that really helps me when I'm stumped for what to say. I made a picture in my mind of myself, sitting in the barber chair. Then I saw picture of myself standing a few feet a away, watching me sitting in the barber chair.

Somehow this kind of "mental distancing" myself from a situation always helps. Sure enough, the right words came to mind.

I said to my target, "Let's see. You're a knock-out in the looks department, you have the great taste to laugh at all my jokes, and you're also very sweet. And life is so unfair that it's got to be the case that you're either married or have a boyfriend, or both."

This got a laugh from everyone present, most importantly her. "Actually, I don't," she said.

By this time, instead of being an embarrassment, it had turned into great entertainment for everyone present, and she was enjoying being the star of the show. You could have cut the silence in that place with the barber's straight razor, as everyone waited to see what the outcome would be.

"Thank you, God", I said, looking heavenward, holding my hands together in mock prayer. Another laugh from all assembled. Then I looked at her, smiled, paused, then said, "I'd be very flattered if you'd have dinner with me tonight." She said, "I'd love to." We set the time, and she gave me her address on a piece of paper and it was one of the most enjoyable and romantic evenings I'd ever had. And her legs felt as good as they looked.

A Last Ditch Method That Will Almost Always Get You A Date Even After A Woman Has Said "No" To Going Out With You

This method will work 9 times out of 10 and really knock a woman out. You should use it only after she's refused your initial offer for a date. I've seen it melt women who had no interest in me whatsoever and initially refused to go out with me.

It works like this. Find out when your waitress, or store clerk, or other working girl is on shift. Go to your local florist and get a nice bouquet of wildflowers and such made up. Don't go for a dozen red roses; that is way too heavy.

Write on the card, "To (Her name), from your secret admirer."

Then have a buddy deliver it on or before her shift. If you can't get a buddy to do it, try to talk a passerby into doing it. People usually enjoy helping out when it is a matter of love. Corny, ain't it?

Wait a few days, before you go for the piece de resistance. Go to your local T-shirt store, and have them make up a T-shirt. It should say, "I AM YOUR SECRET ADMIRER." Put this shirt on under a button up shirt or jacket, and then walk in on your honey pie's shift. Waltz up to her, tap her on the shoulder, and open your shirt or jacket.

Now, that will make an impression. You were clever, different, unique, and went to all that trouble just for her. (Never mind that you only have to pay for the shirt once, but can use it over and over again. Just make sure it stays clean, so it doesn't look used — that will really blow it for you!) After she gets through hugging you, or even kissing you, tell her you'd like to see her, and your willing to go to some effort to do it, and then some. Then ask her out. If she's got any smarts and heart at all, she'll go for it. This is a great, fun method, and it really works like a charm!

By the way, if you don't have a local T-shirt shop, and want to try this, you can order a shirt from me. Specify Small, Medium, Large, or X-tra large, and whether you want the girl's name put on the shirt, so that she knows for sure you did it specially for her, or whether you want the plain, "I AM YOUR SECRET ADMIRER" message. It's twenty bucks, to the same address and same name you sent your original payment for this book.

CHAPTER TEN

SLASHING COMEBACKS FOR SLEAZOID SLUTS!

Women are not always sweet and friendly, dying to meet you, and eager to fulfill your every desire as a man. At times they can be downright nasty.

Who says you have to put up with it, fellas? Here are some wicked replies to her bitchy putdowns, to let her know just who's in charge!

HER: I'M REALLY NOT INTERESTED IN MEETING YOU.

YOU: One of these days you are going to see a man across a room and you're going to want to meet him but it's not going to happen because he's going to intuitively pick up on your incredible capacity for rude behavior.

Alternative One:

YOU: Thank you for showing me how warm and feminine you are.

Alternative Two:

YOU: You've got a little piece of snot hanging out your nose.

Alternative Three:

YOU: (Gazing at her upper lip) Gee. It's amazing what they can do with electrolysis these days.

Alternative Four:

YOU: (pull out a tampon which you should carry for just this purpose) Here. It's gotta be that time of the month!

Alternative Five:

YOU: I'm a lonely person trying to overcome my shyness and you've just slammed me back into my shell for months. I hope you're happy.

Alternative Six:

YOU: Chill out, skirt!

CHAPTER ELEVEN

HOW TO USE THE PERSONALS TO GET HUNDREDS AND HUNDREDS OF WOMEN TO DATE!

Here's how to use the personals to get hundreds and hundreds of responses from just ONE ad! I got over FIVE HUNDRED responses the first time I tried it — you might do even better.

First, DON'T PLACE A PERSONAL AD! Now, I know I seem like I'm contradicting myself here, but please bear with me, because I'm not! If you place a personal ad just like every other guy on the singles page of your local paper, you aren't going to attract the attention that you need! Remember, ATTRACTING ATTENTION IS THE KEY TO MEETING WOMEN!

Instead, place a small classified ad on the singles page of your local paper or magazine. Keep it very simple and don't bother with artwork or fancy trimmings. The paper may do the layout for you for a nominal fee — if not, a graphic artist can do it. If you really want to go cheap, hire an art student from your local college.

Here's how the ad should read:

"WOMEN: How To Find, Win and Keep the Love of Your Life In Thirty Days or Less!

"For absolutely free information send self-addressed stamped envelope to:

"(YOUR ADDRESS GOES IN HERE, DUMMY!)"

You are half-way home now. Instead of a few crummy responses to a personal, you are going to get HUNDREDS and HUNDREDS of women writing! Run the ad two or three times, to convince the skeptics.

Here's the second step. Write a one to two page letter that is a personal ad for you, describing EXACTLY what you want and don't want in a woman. Now of course, I can't tell you what that is. But I can tell you how your letter should start. Do it just like this:

"Dear Reader,

"I have some SHOCKING news for you. You may be just DAYS away from meeting THE LOVE OF YOUR LIFE.

"I have even MORE shocking news for you. You won't have to spend more than 50 cents to meet him, and it shouldn't take more than TEN MINUTES of your time."

I have STILL MORE shocking news for you. Even if this should happen for you, I will still owe you a GREAT, BIG, FAT APOLOGY.

"Allow me a minute to explain.

"This is NOT a pitch for a self-help' book. This is NOT a pitch for a dating service' or one of those disgusting 976' numbers. It's not even a pitch for a seminar, an irresistible love potion, or a psychic astrological-past life love chart.

"So just what the heck IS this a pitch for then?

"Quite simply, dear reader, this is a pitch for ME!

"OK. Allow me ANOTHER minute to explain.

"My name is (your name) and I've gone to the absurd extreme of pulling a crazy stunt like this because I very much want to meet a VERY SPECIAL lady to love and enjoy and respect. Who knows? Maybe YOU are her.

"I KNOW you are out there, somewhere. But I've recently realized that I would have to do something DRASTIC to get your attention, while weeding out all the CRAZIES, LOSERS, and DUM-DUMS who are keeping us from meeting each other.

"I hope that last sentence doesn't seem overly negative, but I think it's a pretty accurate description of the singles scene, for both men AND women."

But I digress .... OK, you get the point. Then go on to describe your good and bad points, what you DON'T want in a woman, and what you do want. Finally, ask them to send a letter and a recent full length photo. If you like what you see, arrange for a meeting.

That's the SMART way to play the personals.

CHAPTER TWELVE

BIRDOGGING

How To Get A Girl When She's With Another Guy (Or When You're With Another Girl)

You're at a party, and so far the action is slow. The classiest girls there are the ones who don't have cookie crumbs in their mustaches. You're seriously considering going home and thumbing through that used copy of Tit and Bum.

And then...in she walks. A stunning raven haired beauty, in tight revealing red dress, her pert breasts straining against the thin, clinging material, nipples jutting, pouting blow job lips parted ever so invitingly. But you notice, to your chagrin, that she's with another guy.

What **will** you do? What will you do??????????????

Here's two approaches for you to use:

APPROACH NUMBER ONE:

As you flit about the room, make casual eye contact with the girl. Try to see from her response if she's interested. If you can't tell, MOVE IN ANYWAY. This is a safe method — he won't get a chance to punch you out. Introduce yourself, TO THE GUY. Be as nice and friendly as you can, and above all KEEP BRINGING THEM BOTH DRINKS. The nastier he should get, the nicer you should be. This increases your stature in her eyes, and decreases his. At some point, Bruiser Boy is going to have to go pee. That's when you make your move. Don't dawdle, for time is of the essence. Move in and pitch for the phone number. Then get out of there fast, before he comes back! Ideally, your bird-dog pitches should be the final ones of the evening as you don't want to be around if she snubs your and then decides to tell him. There are some sicko women who enjoy making their boyfriends angry and jealous. Don't wait to see if she's one of them.

APPROACH NUMBER TWO: Hang out by the Bathroom.

This is generally a good party approach anyway — everyone has to go eventually, and you get a great chance to see what's there in the room. Wait till either your dreamgirl or her beau has to go, and pounce then and there. One thing you should keep in mind — just because a girl is with a guy doesn't mean she's REALLY with the guy. He could be her brother, or cousin, or roommate. If he's really unlucky, he's someone with whom she's "just friends," which, being translated from womanese means, "he takes me everywhere and pays for everything, but if he tries to put a finger on me he'll never see me again." Brutal, aren't they?

CHAPTER THIRTEEN

GETTING THE DATE

OK, let's say you've managed to pick-up a more than passable bimbo. Where do you go from there?

Basically, there are two schools of thought. One school suggests getting her home phone number, waiting a few days to a week, and then calling her for a date.

The other advocates trying to get her to go out with you right then and there, the sooner the better. If you can't get a date with her that evening, you make a date for another time, right on the spot.

I've had both methods work for me, and their are certainly advantages to each. Personally I prefer the on the spot date method. Here's why.

Lots of girls who have nothing otherwise planned will go out with you that night if you make the pitch exciting enough. True, you'd probably like to be with a woman who has more interest in you, but then again we're going to show you techniques to make one of these "got nothing better to do" girls eager to sack with you regardless of their original intentions.

Also, there is something very exciting about going out with a stranger that you just met. It's an air of "anything could happen" that strongly helps to alter a girls mood and make her susceptible to doing things she normally wouldn't.

By way of contrast if you get her home number, and wait several days to call, odds are that the less interested girl is not going to be willing to squeeze you in to her schedule. And you've lost the original excitement of meeting a stranger. So it's up to you. If you like the selling challenge, or just the adrenaline rush of spontaneously making a date on the spot, do it. If you prefer to fight by a set plan, go with the phone number route.

Either way, the next two chapters will show you the winning techniques to pull it off.....

CHAPTER FOURTEEN

GETTING THE PHONE NUMBER ROUTE

If you've ever asked a woman for her phone number, you've probably noticed an interesting phenomena — very few of them say "no" directly. Instead, they say everything BUT "yes."

Have you ever gotten these responses?

"I'm sorry, I don't have a phone." How do you communicate, chick? Smoke signals???

"Why don't you give me your number?" Right. And as soon as your back is turned, that card with your number on it will be shredded so fast the CIA would envy the chick's ability to destroy documents. DON'T BUY IT! If a woman tries this slick trick on you, just nod your head, smile, and walk off, leaving her secure in the knowledge that she met a man too smart for her to bamboozle.

"Sure. It's 555-1212." The old wrong number ploy. Icky, aren't they?

My point is this — if you get anything but her immediate positive response when you ask for her number, you are in big trouble, partner. Giving out the home phone number is a major step into her privacy, and she usually ain't about to do it unless she digs you on SOME level.

What's the best way to ask for the number? Try to be as matter of fact and straightforward as possible. "I'd like to take you out sometime, can I have your home phone number?" will do just fine. If you want to be a little slicker, hand her a pen and a card and say, "Magic seven digits, please." That's a bit more inventive, and inventiveness never hurts.

If you do get the number, get lost as soon as you can. There's no point hanging around after you've closed the sale. Leave her wondering about you and get the hell out of there before you do or say something to make her change her mind.

How long should you wait before you call? That depends. If you sense her interest in you was pretty high, it's safe to wait 5 to 7 days. She'll be wondering what happened and why you haven't called, and that will make you appear more **CHALLENGING** and therefore more attractive in her eyes.

If you sense she wasn't that interested, wait two days and then call.

Muster up all the cheerfulness and fun you can when you make your call to pitch the date. You want to sound carefree, fun, and excited about the absolute blast the two of you are going to have together. Talk to her in the tone of voice you'd use for an old friend who you enjoy being with.

The key point is to ask her out **FOR A SPECIFIC NIGHT.** Don't say, "Would you like to get together this week?" or "What night are you free?" That's a weak pitch. You want to come on stronger than that.

Use "Let's have dinner Wednesday night, eight o'clock. Then we can go dancing." Then **SHUT YOUR MOUTH AND DO NOT SAY A WORD!!!!!**

That brief moment of silence is the acid test. If you hear a long hesitation before she answers, or excuses, or anything but, "Sure, I'd love too," you've got a problem on your hands.

If a woman really does want to see you, but has something to do on the night you've asked her to be with you, and just can't cancel those plans, what will her response be? **SHE'LL MAKE A COUNTER-OFFER.** Something on the lines of, "I can't Wednesday, but how about Thursday at 8 o'clock?"

Don't confuse a counter-offer with an "I'm busy, but how about another time?" That's a stone cold REJECTION. If she really wanted to go out with you another time, she'd tell you when that time is. Take it from someone who used to fall for this one all the time — it will do nothing but generate useless, time-wasting wishful thinking on your part. Either you get the date, or a specific counter-offer, or you FORGET IT!

One final warning here, because women are even trickier than you can imagine. Often times you'll make your pitch for a specific night to go out; say a Wednesday. And you'll hear, "That's sounds like fun. Sure I'll go."

Then, throbbing with the thrill of victory, as you are about to hang up you hear, "Oh. Could you do me a favor? Could you call back Wednesday about 6 pm to confirm?" Or you might hear, "Call me Wednesday around 6 pm and I'll give you my address."

DON'T GET SUCKERED BY THIS TRICK! You haven't got a date in this instance, you have an option for a date, which is about as valuable as an IOU from one of my gambling buddies who live at the race track. The chick is waiting to hear from the guy she's REALLY interested in, and if he's not available, then you may get the date.

If a girl tries to pull this on you, say something like, "I don't think that's a good idea. We'll try another time when your schedule is looser."

That will put her in her place nicely. You've shown her that you can't be suckered and she can't call the shots — almost certainly an unlikely and unusual occurrence. That will definitely get her attention.

Wait a week and call her back. Chances are she'll accept the date without the "call and confirm" bullshit. If she doesn't, then **TOSS HER NUMBER AWAY** and move on to the next adventure. She's just out to waste your time anyway.

Once you've made your date with your lady, get off the phone! Again, you might blow it if you stay on and jabber, and you want to keep her wondering about you. Do your talking on the date! If you hit it off on the phone, where does that leave you? You can't get laid over a phone wire, whatever the 976 numbers would have you believe! Save it for the date.

Finally, nowadays almost everyone has one of those damn phone answering machines! **DO NOT LEAVE A MESSAGE ON ONE OF THESE BEFORE YOU'VE HAD A DATE WITH A WOMAN.** Using a phone machine as a buffer between you and the lady is weak, anti-challenge, and puts the ball in her court, as you either have to wait for her to call you back or alternatively, look impatient and desperate by calling her to see if she got your message. **AVOID THIS PHONE BLUNDER LIKE THE PLAGUE!**

BASIC PHONE PITCHING RULES:

1. DO TRY TO USE A HAPPY, CAREFREE, EAGER TO HAVE ALL THIS FUN TOGETHER TONE OF VOICE.

2. ASK HER OUT FOR A SPECIFIC NIGHT.

3. DON'T FALL FOR "OPTION DATES."

4. HANG UP AS SOON AS YOU POLITELY CAN, ONCE YOU'VE MADE THE DATE.

5. DO NOT UNDER ANY, ANY, ANY, ANY CIRCUM- STANCES WHATSOEVER LEAVE A MESSAGE WITH HER ANSWERING MACHINE OR A ROOMMATE EITHER FOR THAT MATTER. THE FIRST TIME YOU TALK TO HER PERSON TO PERSON IS THE FIRST TIME YOU'VE EVER CALLED, AS FAR AS SHE SHOULD KNOW.

CHAPTER FIFTEEN

MAKING THE DATE ON THE SPOT

This is the method I think is the best. There's something exciting and spontaneous about it that you just can't get using the phone number method.

The thing to keep in mind here is to try to appear casual. You don't want it to look like you are dying to rush her back to your place and rip her panties off.

The best illustration of this method was given to me recently by a friend of mine, Jim. Here's the story he told me:

"Our regular secretary at work was going to be gone for a few days, so we wanted to hire someone temporary, just to answer phones. Someone was scheduled to come by that afternoon, and the boss was going to be out of the office. He told me if I liked her, I could go ahead and hire her.

"She was a cute little blonde named Megan. She came in about 4:30 in the afternoon. We talked for a while, and I told her she had the job. Then I invited her to go next door for coffee.

"Well, we talked for about an hour and then I asked her if she wanted to have dinner. We did, and that turned into a movie. And from there we went back to my place and did all sorts of wonderfully obscene things to each other for several hours."

Here's the main point: Try to steer the girl you've just met into a different environment. Don't make it elaborate- anywhere nearby will do. The corner Yogurt stand for some frozen fermented cow juice; the local pizza parlor, even a bowling alley. You want a chance to set her down and use the mood altering hypnotic techniques we're going to be showing you.

Whatever you do, don't invite her back to your place right away, or do anything that might scare her off. Make it seem like you just want to spend fifteen minutes talking in a public place. With what we are going to show you, that's all you are going to need.

CHAPTER SIXTEEN

HOW TO HANDLE CHICKS WHO TRY TO CANCEL DATES

Perhaps the most serious offense a chick can commit is to cancel a date. I've heard all sorts of hilarious excuses, and nine times out of ten they are just that.

But so what? With the proper amount of coercion and psychological pressure, you can get her to go out with you anyway. Then you can use one of the quick-lay/hypnosis tricks we'll show you so you can **still** wind up screwing her. How dare she try to waste the time of a master of Guerilla Get Laid tactics? As Batman would say, "Poor deluded girl!"

It's really quite simple. When she calls to cancel with her silly excuse, you just do this:

HER: Oh, I'm sorry, but I can't make it tonight. I have to take my friend to the airport (Or: "I'm just not feeling well," or whatever lie she tells you).

YOU: So what you're saying is, you'd like to go, but due to a circumstance you can't control and weren't expecting, you won't be able to?

HER: Yeah. That's right. (She's **got** to admit this — she can't come right out and say she just isn't interested. That might take a little guts.)

YOU: (Closing in for the kill) Well, since you said you'd like to go, what arrangements would you like to make to do that right now?

Then, you shut up. You have the silly chick. She's backed into a corner, and will have to name a day, or else risk being revealed as the liar she truly is.

Your other option is to blow the chick off, but make it as embarrassing and uncomfortable for her as is humanly possible.

Here is a **great** way to make her feel absolutely awful:.

HER: Oh, I can't make our date because my parrot is having an existential crisis and I want to see him through it.

YOU: Hmm. You know, I'm sitting here, with the phone in my hand, listening to you speak, and I realize I **still** don't understand what's going on. And I also realize I can accept hearing the full and complete truth from you. So, why don't you tell me **again** what's going on.

It's very important that you say that last sentence with the right inflection and tonality. You're implying a part of the sentence which isn't actually said which is, "...and this time tell me the **truth**."

Believe it or else, but nine times out of ten, the chick actually will fess up and admit her deception. That's when you pounce on her!

YOU: So, how does it feel to know that you're afraid to take responsibility for your own decisions and have to resort to lying about them?

Oh, the joy of battle, my brothers! Flushing a chick down the toilet of humiliation is almost as great a kick as scoring!

Now, once in a while, a chick will cancel, but when she does she'll make a counter-offer to go out again another time. This at least is better than a straight cancellation without such an offer, but I'd strongly advise <u>against</u> accepting. She could be just throwing you a bone to make you feel better, but even if she isn't, your accepting her offer of doing it another time **makes you look too easily available and removes the element of your being a challenge to her.** This will make you look <u>much</u> less appealing in her eyes.

Here's the right way to handle this. Let's say you have a date for Saturday, and she calls you Friday evening.

HER: I'm sorry, but I really can't make it Saturday. I've got friends coming in from out of town. But I really do want to see you. Can we go out Sunday instead?

YOU: No, I have plans for Sunday (even if you don't and you are dying to be with her — bite the bullet and refuse!).

At this point you have two options:

Option One

YOU: Why don't we try another time when your schedule is a little looser?

Then politely say goodbye, and hang-up. Wait 2 weeks, then call and ask her out for a specific night. If she doesn't accept or make a specific counter-offer, toss the number and move on.

Option Two

YOU: Well, I'll tell you, this is just the way it is for me. It's just the way I do things. When I make a date, and someone cancels, I leave it up to them to make the next date. So, if you want to go out, I'm interested. Call me, and I'll say yes.

Personally, I prefer this option. It's not as down and dirty as the first one, but it is effective nonetheless. By putting the ball back in her court, you don't have to spend the two weeks before you call, wondering if she's really interested (you shouldn't be wondering this, but it's hard to have that kind of discipline, and I'm a sucker for situations that I can't quite figure out). You can just safely assume she <u>isn't</u> interested, forget about her, and leave it up to her to pleasantly surprise you. And you also preserve the element of being a challenge, conveying the all important message **I DON'T NEED <u>YOU</u>, <u>YOU</u> NEED <u>ME</u>.**

OK. Now you're ready for the ultimate secrets. In the next chapters we're going to be showing you how, just by talking to a woman, you can get her so damned turned on during the date that she'll be itching to screw you. Hang on to your hats, gentlemen.

PART THREE

HOW TO GET THE WOMEN YOU DATE INTO BED

CHAPTER SEVENTEEN

DECIDING YOUR APPROACH

The next few chapters will emphasize quick-lay strategies: How To Score on the First Date or even sooner than that!

However, you may decide that you want something more than quick, hot sex with a girl. If you want a relationship with a lady, I recommend that you don't use the techniques in the next few chapters.

CHAPTER EIGHTEEN

HOW TO USE HYPNOSIS TO GET YOUR DATE INTO THE SACK

What you are about to read may stretch your ability to believe to the breaking point. I don't blame you for having that reaction at all.

All I can tell you is that this stuff works - it works so well that it scares me at times. My only comfort is knowing that as you become more and more successful and powerful with women, you lose the desire to abuse the power. Success makes you want to go a little bit easy on the poor defenseless creatures.

What I am about to show you will allow you to create very powerful feelings of being turned on and excited in almost any woman you can spend time with. You don't have to rely on luck, or that special "chemistry" or "spark." This chapter will show you how to create that in about ten minutes time, with almost any woman you want, in almost any circumstances. Instead of dates that end up with a polite peck on the cheek, you'll end up taking it as far as you want to go, regardless of how the woman felt about you before you used these techniques on her.

One last caution before I lay out this technology. In some states, rape is defined as "intercourse of a woman, by a man, by force, threat of force, or OTHERWISE WITHOUT CONSENT." In some states, if you get a date drunk, and fuck her when she's passed out, you could find yourself facing a rape rap.

Likewise for hypnosis. I am not an attorney, and am not going to give you legal advice, but I warn you here and now of the possible consequences and am not about to be held responsible if you get slapped with charges. YOU USE THESE METHODS AT YOUR OWN RISK (And I wouldn't have to give this disclaimer/warning if these methods didn't work as well as they do).

HOW IT ALL WORKS:

COVERT HYPNOSIS AND THE STRUCTURE OF SEDUCTION

This method works because **it bypasses all of a woman's conscious resistance to screwing you.** It doesn't matter what that conscious resistance is based on. Maybe you are not her type and she THINKS she needs a certain LOOK in a guy to turn her on. Maybe she wants you but is afraid of looking cheap if she comes across too fast. Maybe she's just recently been burned by a guy and isn't eager to have it happen again.

It DOESN'T matter why, because **from now on you will be able to get past all of that by bypassing her CONSCIOUS mind and getting right to her UNCONSCIOUS.** If this sounds like bull, please stick with me for just a few more pages, because what you are about to see is a MAGIC key for getting laid with startling frequency.

SCORING TECHNIQUE NUMBER ONE:

STACKING REALITIES

Let me tell you a story about my buddy, Rick. Rick told me about this experience he had whenever he read a book. As he was reading along, he could begin to be aware of certain things. As he read, he could suddenly be aware of the unique darkness and shape of the letters. And as he became aware of that, he could also see the contrasting whiteness of the page. And he could also be aware of the smoothness of the paper. And as he became aware of that, he could also feel the rise and fall of his chest as he breathed, and the slightest little nodding, little nodding of his head. And as his eyes began to close ....

Now, what just happened as you were reading that? Even though I'm not standing over your shoulder as you read this, I'll bet my Batman comic book collection, that you started to notice the things I was talking about. You noticed the darkness of the letters, the brightness of the page, and the smoothness of the paper. And you noticed your breathing and your eyes started to close.

Here's the point: The only way to understand something you are hearing or reading, **is by having a little bit of the experience yourself. Naturally, and without any resistance, you began to experience what I wanted you to, because you had to do so in order to make sense out of my words.**

But notice something else of CRITICAL IMPORTANCE. I didn't suggest that you experience these things, or warn you in advance, or give you a direct command. **That would have caused immense resistance on your part.** Instead, I presented it to you as part of a story. **I told you about an experience SOMEONE ELSE HAD, AND THE ONLY WAY FOR YOU TO UNDERSTAND THAT WAS TO HAVE THE EXPERIENCE FOR YOURSELF.**

This is the same pattern and technique that you can use to put a woman into an altered state and get her to feel and do just about whatever you'd like her to. You start by telling her a story about someone else, and that story describes an experience that involves the feelings and actions you want HER to take. It sounds too simple and too good to be true, but it WORKS! And the more you practice the better you get.

Let's do a sample of this, to let you see just exactly how to use this technique that she'll be unable to resist. You may want to wait till later in the evening, when you are alone in your apartment.

Even though it usually only takes five minutes or so, you still don't want to run the risk of being interrupted.

After the usual small talk, here's how it would go:

YOU: Hey, did I tell you yet about my friend, Mike?

HER: No. What about him?

YOU: Well, this is interesting. I remember one time Mike told me this story. You see, he had this friend. And this friend noticed something unusual when she'd listen to someone talk. Like for example she could become aware of the sound of his voice .... and as she heard the sound of his voice, she could also hear the other sounds of people in the room .... and she could become aware .... of the rising and falling of her chest .... and the slight nodding of her head as she listened .... and the deep, deep richness of his voice .... and as she became aware .... of all these things .... the pressure of her hand as it rested on the table .... and the outline of his face as she watched him speak .... her attention would become riveted .... on a very unique detail of his face .... whatever it might be that seemed to capture her attention .... so that as she focused more and more on this part of his face .... she became more and more fascinated by what he had to say .... more and more captivated and totally enraptured by this experience of him that she was having .... and as she allowed herself to realize these things .... she could also feel a deep longing within herself for him .... to feel his touch .... his gentle touch across her face. (Reach and gently stroke her with the back of your hand) .... and as she felt this touch and her eyes closed with the pleasure of it .... her breathing began to deepen, and her heart began to pound .... to pound .... with the rich .... deep warmth of his voice .... the rich, deep warmth that began to spread .... began to pound through her chest .... and through her belly .... and deep through her thighs .... as the warmth and the wetness and the deep rich pounding of her most burning female place .... the pounding burning place .... that longed to be filled, ached to be filled .... filled with his throbbing rock-hard manness .... and as she felt these things .... deeper and deeper and even more intensely .... the feeling of his hand as it touched her thigh... let her know that she would open herself to this man completely .... give herself to him .... at the time he chose to take her ....

Now .... I guarantee that THAT WILL GET you laid .... if she doesn't rape you right there .... just make sure you repeat that same touch you gave her on the thigh, later on in the evening.

In hypnosis terms, this is known as an anchor. Basically, all that means is that when a person has an experience, anything that is associated or linked with that experience will cause the person to recall the entire experience. It's what Pavlov did to his dogs — by associating the ringing of a bell with the state of hunger and drooling, he could set of that state by simply ringing the bell at any time thereafter. In this case, you are also ringing someone's bell, but hopefully she will NOT BE A DOG!!!

You'll have to decide when to use this approach. You can use it in the restaurant or wait until after when she's in your apartment. It depends on how daring you want to get.

FIRST DATE SCREW TECHNIQUE TWO:

ANCHORING

We mentioned anchoring above, briefly, and here's another way to use it to get laid on the first date.

The first step to making this work is to find out your date's preferred representational system. (FOR A DETAILED GUIDE TO DOING THIS, SEE APPENDIX TWO AT THE END OF THIS BOOK.) You find this out by asking her to recall her last vacation and have her describe in her own words, what she liked best. If she says she enjoyed the feeling of laying out in the sun, and swimming in the warm waves, you've got a kinesthetic person. If she says she liked the sound of the pounding surf, and the quiet nights, she's auditory. If she uses visual terms, she's visual.

Next, ask if she can remember the most exciting experience she's had recently. When you say the word "exciting" drop your voice a bit, and give it an erotic connotation. Nine out of ten times a woman will recall an erotic experience.

When she answers yes, ask her to close her eyes a minute. Then, depending on what her preferred system is, ask her to remember, what she saw, what she heard, and how it felt in her body. As she experiences this, you'll notice things start to change. Her face will flush, her breathing will get heavy, her lower lip will get larger, and she will actually re-experience in her body all those lovely erotic feelings she had when she first went through the experience.

As she's doing this, tell her that when those feelings in her body reach their peak, she should wiggle her pink finger. When she wiggles it, reach over and give her right wrist a squeeze, and at the same time, say, "Good." Run her through this a two more times.

Then have her clear her mind, and close her eyes. Reach over, squeeze her wrist, and say good. If you've done it right, she'll go right back into the erotic state she was in before.

Now, tease her with it. Go back to normal conversation, then a minute later, reach over and trigger the anchor again. Look into her eyes, and smile at her as your do it, but this time, don't let go of her wrist. Keep squeezing, keeping her in the erotic state until you stop.

You now have a weapon you can use any time during the rest of the evening!

Later in the evening, when your get her back at your place, tease her a bit. Don't make a pass for a long time, just smile knowingly. If she makes a comment you think is interesting, reach over, squeeze the wrist, and say "good."

When she goes into the erotic state again, keep one hand on the wrist squeezing, then attack with the free hand and your mouth.

Practice anchoring. You'll get better at it and it does take some practice - we shouldn't kid ourselves about that. But shit — it works nicely!

What's great about this technique and the previous technique of stacking realities is you often don't have to go on a formal date. You can take a girl you just met for an innocent cup of coffee and get her ready to fuck you in fifteen minutes time. Why waste time going out when you could be going in?

FIRST DATE SCREW TECHNIQUE THREE:

SENSORY OVERLAP

Again to make this work, you have to find out the lady's preferred system.

Once you do that, you start talking to her about the beach. You start by asking her to recall something from her preferred system about the beach.

Let's say you are talking to a woman who's preferred system is auditory. Here's how you'd do it:

YOU: Hey, let's try an imagination experiment. Close your eyes for a second. Let's take an imaginary trip to the beach. You're at the beach. And you can hear the sound of the wind as it blows, and the sound of the waves .... and the sound of a gull, crying overhead .... and as you hear the sound of the waves .... (switch to visual system) you can also see a wave as it moves toward the shore .... you can see the sunlight glinting off the wave, and some of the white spray that's being blown off by the wind .... and as you see that spray .... you can also feel it gently touch your face now .... and as you feel the spray on your face .... and the rise and fall of your chest as you breath .... and the gentle warmth of the sun on your face .... you can begin to feel a deep and comfort and warmth .... and a feeling of being totally at ease.

(Here's where you get her. You've already hypnotized her, because when you switch people from their preferred system to a system that is normally not in their conscious awareness, they enter an altered state) .... and that feeling of ease and warmth, begins to spread through your body .... with each breath you take .... the rise and fall of your chest .... allows a glowing rich warmth to spread throughout your body .... a warmth that feels so very good .... so good .... like warm and gentle hands .... massaging throughout your body .... (from here you lead her in the same manner as the first stacking realities technique).

MORE POWER CLOSES FOR GETTING YOU LAID

I want to emphasize again the important super-rule you should make part of you. I want you to eat, sleep, breathe and shit this rule:

I MAKE NO EXCUSES FOR MY DESIRES AS A MAN

This rule is important in every aspect of dealing with a woman, but no where more so than when you make that first serious pass.

If you aren't going to use the hypnotic techniques mentioned in the previous chapters, then I suggest you use one or both of the following power closes.

POWER CLOSE ONE:

TAKING WHAT BELONGS TO YOU CLOSE

What does the average guy do when a woman invites him into her apartment for a cup of coffee?

I'll tell you what he does. He makes small talk while the coffee is brewing, all the while sweating and nervous about when he's going to make his pass.

Then, when she serves the coffee, he drinks it nervously, wondering when he should make a move. Maybe they sit down on the couch, and he wonders when he should sit closer.

Time wears on. Nothing has happened, and he's getting more and more out of control. Maybe he spills his drink or has to keep going to the bathroom.

Perhaps he decides he better do something, so he moves a little closer and kind of apologetically puts an arm around her. He starts to slowly finger her hair, waiting to see her response.

The first power close cuts through all that nonsense Here's how it works.

She invites you in for coffee. You let her slide while the coffee is brewing. This is her safe time - the last few minutes she'll EVER be safe around you again. You can chuckle to yourself as you look at her and realize that.

The coffee is ready and she pours it for both of you. After she takes the first sip, don't say anything. Just suddenly stop talking and look at her intensely, with just the slightest hint of a smile.

At this point she'll notice, and probably ask, what is it. You CALMLY, SLOWLY, AND DELIBERATELY, put your cup down, reach over, take hers out of her hand, and put it down. Look at her for a second, take her face in her hands, and kiss her passionately.

This kind of action is sending a woman a POWERFUL message about the kind of man you are. You are in effect saying, WITHOUT WORDS, "Let's skip the crap baby. I want you, HERE, NOW, AND I'M NOT MAKING ANY EXCUSES FOR IT."

This is my favorite, non-hypnotic close, although I can't entirely call it that, because women seem to go into a trance with the slow, deliberate, but unexpected movements you make.

A key to making this pitch work is SAYING NOTHING! If you talk, you've ruined it! Also, your movements must be slow, and deliberate, not hurried and rushed, like you are afraid she's going to stop you.

POWER CLOSE NUMBER TWO:
THE TEASE

With this close, you operate as if you absolutely knew the girl wanted to desperately sleep with you, but you are determined to hold out till the last possible minute and to enjoy teasing her all evening.

With this approach, you lean into her as you talk as if you are about to kiss her. Then you MOVE AWAY. Get up and fix yourself a drink, or go to the bathroom. When you play with her mind like this, she won't know what to think. And when you put her in that state of mind, she's much more pliable and less likely to resist you.

A good tactic is to wait until she says something funny, and then reach over and brush the side of her face with the OUTSIDE of your hand. Then say something like, "You're such a funny lady." Do this slowly and deliberately, looking in her eyes the whole time. Then PULL AWAY.

Here's how you end this. While you're talking, suddenly yawn, look at your watch, and say, "I'm feeling a little bushed. Let's call it an evening."

If you're at your place, you proceed like this: "C'mon. I'll drive you home." Make as if you're really getting to leave. As she stands up from the couch, take her in your arms, and kiss her passionately. It's the last thing she'll be expecting, and the unexpected has the best effect.

THE MAKE OUT

When you are making out with a lady, you want to show her that you are determined and powerful and certain you will get what you want.

Don't waste too much time in her mouth. This is where most men make their big error. Go for her neck as soon as you can. As you go for her neck, cup her breast in one of your hands. Gently rub it with the palm of your hand.

Let your hands roam freely over her legs and ass — you are the rightful king, and this is YOUR TERRITORY, rightfully yours to explore as you see fit.

Rather than trying to get your hands in her pants right away, take the palm of your hand, and place it over her pubic mound. If you press down lightly and move your palm up and down you will get her very hot and bothered.

Don't bother trying to take off her bra either, before you take her breasts in your mouth. Simply lift up her shirt or blouse, and pull the cup of the bra down, so the breast is exposed. Lick, AROUND the nipple at first, instead of going at it directly.

Then, let your tongue flick it quickly a few times. Then bite it .... not hard enough to hurt.

If she's wearing pants, move your head down, and kiss her on the crotch. Then reach for her belt, if she's wearing one, and undo. Don't be shy about it. Pull her pants right off, and try to take her panties with them, if you can.

Kiss back up to her chest now, but this time you work your palm on her naked bush, slipping your index finger on her clit, and in her cunt.

After a few minutes of this, move back down to her pussy. Kiss her inner thighs once or twice and then go for the eat-out.

Here is my favorite cunnilingus technique. I discovered it by accident years ago, and women go crazy over it. I don't claim to be the best fuck in the world — I know I am not. However, women have told me, over and over again that I give the best head of any man they have ever met.

Here's the secret. Kneel down so your face is level with her snatch. She can sit on the edge of the bed or chair or couch, with her legs over your shoulders. Take the index finger of your left hand, and the index finger of your right hand. Use the left finger to push away the skin hiding the clitoris on that side, and the right finger to push away the skin hiding the clitoris on the other. Once you've pushed this loose skin to the side the clitoris will be exposed. From here, what you do is use your fingers to push the base of the clitoris, so it pops up, fully exposed. This is sort of the equivalent of a woman squeezing the base of your cock when she blows you — it helps to keep your cock rigid by trapping the blood in it and also keeps it from moving.

From here, she's yours. You'll be able to suck and lick on the little bingo button and she'll freak out. The hardest problem will be getting her to hold still — if she thrashes around too much you are going to lose your grip.

At this point, stop for a minute and take off your pants and shorts. Resume eating, and when you feel ready, roll on your condom. You should practice this until you can do it quickly and without fumbling.

Then spread her legs open and slip it in slow and deep. Let her enjoy the pleasure of having your cock inside of her.

CHAPTER NINETEEN

HOW TO TOTALLY BREAK A WOMAN'S RESISTANCE TO SLEEPING WITH YOU

We've all heard the nonsense about "No Means No" and respecting a girl's right to refuse a pass.

Well, I hope by now you know differently. Often times "no" doesn't mean that at all. It could mean, "I don't want to appear cheap, so I have to put up token resistance first." Or it could mean, "I'm not sure." Or it could mean, "I'm scared of sex."

Whatever it means, the two worst responses you could make to a woman who resists you, are to:

1. Argue with her about it.

2. Give up and sulk.

The best thing to do is express agreement with how she feels, then back off and try later again in the evening. If she's just trying to avoid appearing easy or cheap, you'll nail her later anyway.

The real problem arises when the lady just happens to have a serious problem about sex or is just NOT attracted to you.

In the first case, you are in trouble, buddy. If she's this hung up, what kind of a fuck is she going to be anyway? Personally, I'd see her to the door and throw away her phone number.

If she's not attracted to you, but likes sex generally, you've still got a fighting chance. Let me show you several ways around the, "I'M JUST NOT ATTRACTED TO YOU LINE."

METHOD ONE: AS IF FRAME

This is perhaps the sneakiest and most unfair method I know to break a woman's resistance to sleeping with you. It is the H-bomb in your arsenal. It works on the principle that if you put someone in the physiology of a certain state, they will actually BE in that state.

Here's how it works. You make the pass and she rejects you. You should act apologetic. Tell her you are sorry you misread her cues. Say something like, "Look. I'm sorry. I'm just really dumb when it comes to reading women, y'know. Maybe you can help me with this? I know this sounds really dumb, but I don't want to keep making this kind of dumb mistake with women."

Odds are, she'll be willing to help.

"If you can remember a time you were with a guy that you were really attracted to, can you show me what the look was on your face?"

She'll laugh at first, but then show you.

"OK. But can you show me how your mouth was? Was it open? And how did your eyes look?"

"OK. And how were you breathing? Can you show me?"

"How were you sitting? What was your posture?"

"And what feelings, closing your eyes for a second, were you aware of in your body? And how did those start to build?"

At this point, you have a choice. You can anchor those feelings and make a pass later by firing off the anchor, or you can make a pass then and there, using a transition like this:

"And how would this touch feel to you if he were touching you like this, here and now?" Resume your pass now.

METHOD TWO: REDEFINE THE MEANING OF THE SITUATION

This is a more verbal approach than the last method. When she feeds you the "I'm just not attracted to you" objection, you reply as follows:

"What you're really saying is you have an unprecedented opportunity to expand the range of people you can share joy and pleasure with."

That will blow her mind. You've taken a negative and turned it around into a positive opportunity for her to grow and expand her life. You've made her excuse for not fucking you her positive reason to do so. Wow!

METHOD THREE: CONSEQUENCES

Here you point out the consequences of her actions by saying: "Telling me that is only going to make me want you more, because I get really turned on when women reject me." Well, where does THAT leave her? You've let her know that pushing you away again is only going to make it worse for her! She can't win no matter what.

METHOD FOUR: SHOCK

This method relies on interrupting her pattern by reversing the tables. Here you say: "Attracted? Who says I'M attracted to YOU. As far as I'm concerned, honey, I'm giving you a MERCY fuck!" Then immediately resume your pass.

METHOD FIVE: HUMOR

Here you interrupt her pattern of rejection again, but this time more gently. Politely say, "Oh. I'm sorry. Excuse me." Then get up, and go into the kitchen. Get a paper shopping bag, stick it on your head, and walk back over to her. "There," you say, "that should fix it!" As she laughs, resume your pass.

METHOD SIX: GUILT

One of the hardest things for anyone to do is watch a grown man cry. You are going to depend on that for this method, but be aware that this one is going to take some acting ability. Pull away after she rejects you and put your head in your hands. Quietly start to sob. "I'm sorry .... I should have known better than to think .... that a girl like you .... could like me .... " Sob some more. "Let me sit a second .... and I'll take you home." (Obviously if you are at HER place, you word it accordingly, dummy!) "It's just that I'll never know .... the peace .... of having you in my arms .... and loving you .... it would have meant so much .... (sob, sob). I've never been with a woman as beautiful as you .... you don't know the confidence it would have given me...and the happiness .... . (sob uncontrollably now) .... could you find it in yourself .... just to let me kiss you once .... to know I at least had that?"

Now I promise you, if the girl has any heart at ALL, she'll kiss you. And that's when you resume your pass. If she stops you, start weeping again.

CHAPTER TWENTY

A FINAL WORD

Well, we've come a long way together. You've learned and hopefully applied methods to give you unbeatable and easy confidence with women. You know how to meet women left and right, and how to score with the ones you want, when and where YOU want to.

I sincerely hope that you put the techniques in this book to use. Make them WORK for you. You'll be astonished at how easily and quickly they can bring you success and happiness with women.

I've been a colossal failure with women and a colossal success and you know what? Colossal success is not only one hell of a lot more fun, it's also one hell of a lot easier! Once you know how to do it, it's HARD to fail with women, and EASY to get what you want.

I hope you discover just how easy it is! And how much nicer colossal success can be!

ROSS JEFFRIES, LOS ANGELES, CALIFORNIA

APRIL 1989

Author's Final Note

To recieve your Ross Jeffries "Get Laid" Catalog ABSOLUTE FREE, write or call: Straightforward, 11918 Millpond Court, Manassas VA 22111-3283, 1.703.791.6421

You will recieve a catalog chocked full of great stuff and its all guaranteed to get you laid or we don't get paid. Yes, one full year guarantee of all products in the Ross Jeffries Catalog.

Get Laid Like Crazy with these Ross Jeffries Audio Tapes

The Advanced Ross Jeffries Training Collection:

<u>Sex Seminars Audios</u> ... (3 tapes approximately 3 1/2 hours) In these live, uncensored tapes, recorded from two separate seminars, Ross covers some of his advanced, latest techniques for meeting and seducing women, and dramatically increasing you personal power. Topics include:

☛ How to instantly put yourself into an incredibly powerful state of mind to attract women to you <u>automatically</u>

☛ The 4 major attitudes of the "super studs" and how to make them part of your own personality AUTOMATICALLY

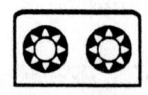

☛ Brand new techniques for erasing past failures and putting you old, limited self on the shelf

☛ The AIRIP formula for meeting and picking up women anywhere!

☛ A super-clever technique that will literally have women lining up to meet you wherever you go, using something that fits in the palm of you hand!!! (This is no joke, and Ross considers it the best technique for meeting women he's ever seen!)

☛ Power Questions: How to use the questions you ask yourself to guide you to unstoppable seduction moves!!!

☛ How to break out of a slump and go into an unstoppable winning streak, seducing girl after gorgeous girl, using insights and secrets from professional gambling experts

and much much more! These tapes are not only chocked full of the <u>latest, cutting edge</u> seduction TECHNOLOGY, but are also hilariously funny! So be prepared to get laid and laugh your ass off as Ross teaches in his entertaining, unimitable style. (Warning: these tapes are uncensored, and contain vulgar language!) **Live Sex Seminar Audios – RJ26 – $39.95**

APPENDIX ONE

THE ULTIMATE RULES AND ATTITUDES FOR SUCCESS WITH WOMEN

Note: These attitudes and rules are the foundation of everything in this book, and the key to your success with women. To make them work for you, you must practice them, both in your imagination and real life! Write them down on three by five index cards, and visualize yourself putting them into action.

Attitude/Rule One:

I MAKE NO EXCUSES FOR MY DESIRES AS A MAN-
I MOVE THROUGH THE WORLD
WITHOUT APOLOGY

Attitude/Rule Two:

I DON'T NEED YOU-YOU NEED ME

Attitude/Rule Three:

YOU CAN'T CONTROL ME

Attitude/Rule Four:

I NEVER KNOW WHERE I STAND WITH A WOMAN
UNTIL I MAKE THAT FIRST SERIOUS PASS, SO
I DON'T CONSIDER A WOMAN A
SERIOUS PROSPECT
UNTIL AFTER WE'VE MADE LOVE

Attitude/Rule Five:

THE FIRST STEP IN ATTRACTING A WOMAN IS
GETTING HER ATTENTION,
AND THE BEST WAY TO DO THAT
IS BY BEING UNIQUE, AND NOVEL, AND
DIFFERENT

Attitude/Rule Six:

I DON'T ARGUE WITH A WOMAN AND NEITHER DO I ATTEMPT TO APPEASE HER. I LISTEN CAREFULLY TO WHAT SHE HAS TO SAY, BUT GENTLY AND FIRMLY DO AS I HAD PLANNED ALL ALONG

Attitude/Rule Seven:

THERE IS NO WOMAN SO BEAUTIFUL THAT I CAN'T MAKE HER MINE

Attitude/Rule Eight:

A "5" IN YOUR BED BEATS A "10" IN YOUR HEAD, BUT A "10" IN YOUR BED, BEATS A HUNDRED "5's" IN YOUR HEAD!

Attitude/Rule Nine:

NEVER GET SERIOUSLY INVOLVED WITH A WOMAN WHO HAS MORE PROBLEMS THAN YOU DO

Attitude/Rule Ten:

PERSISTENCE WITHOUT FLEXIBILITY IS A PRESCRIPTION FOR DISASTER. VARY YOUR APPROACH AND STYLE TO DISCOVER WHAT WORKS THE BEST

APPENDIX TWO

REPRESENTATIONAL SYSTEMS

People perceive the world in three basic modes: Visual (pictures), Auditory (sounds), Kinesthetic (body feelings). While everyone uses one or more of these systems at any given time, most people have a preferred system. If you speak to them using terms from their preferred system, you will create great feelings of rapport and warmth, because you are, in effect, speaking to them in the language their brain prefers.

How To Find Out Your Date's Preferred System

Step One: Ask, "Can you recall the last time you had a really fun vacation?"

Step Two: After getting a "yes" answer, ask, "What did you really like most about it?"

Step Three: Make sure your date uses SENSORY terms to describe the experience. If she just says, "It was really fun!" you haven't gotten anywhere. Ask her what specifically about it was fun.

Step Four: Listen for the sensory based terms she uses to describe the experience. "I really liked the water. It was so clear and blue. And you could see the bits of sunlight sparkling off the tops of the waves." Guess what? She's visual.

Step Five: Describe a recent experience of yours to her, using terms from her preferred system.

Step Six: Watch her non-verbal responses as you describe your experience. You should notice, if you are really getting through to her, pupil dilation (her eyes getting big and wide, dumdum), increased breathing rate, etc.

APPENDIX THREE

INDUCING TRANCE STATES IN YOUR DATE USING THE STORY TELLING METHOD

First, never, NEVER mention that you can do this! If you tell her about it, you might as well forget about it! Don't say the word "hypnosis" — it will have the same affect as saying "AIDS" or "Herpes." Your aim is not to impress with what you know, but to use what you know to get results!

Try to do this in a quiet place.

STEP ONE: Find out your date's preferred system. This isn't absolutely necessary for this particular method, but it sure can help!

STEP TWO: Start by telling a story, but make the story hard to follow. You want to overwhelm her conscious ability to keep track. Thus you would say, "Did I ever tell you about my friend, Jim? It seems he was at this conference, and he was in the hotel bar on a break. And the bartender was telling a story about his neighbor who had two brothers. One was really good at dealing with people, but the other had problems until he met this guy." etc, etc.

STEP THREE: Weave elements of your current situation into the story that are based on your dates current sensory experience.

STEP FOUR: Lead her into a kinesthetic mode of experience and describe erotic body sensations.

STEP FIVE: Make a smooth transition into your physical pass at her. Don't suddenly stop talking and roughly grab her. You'll jolt her out of the state you worked so hard to build.

APPENDIX FOUR

THE RIGHT WAY TO USE VISUALIZATION TO BUILD IRRESISTIBLE CONFIDENCE

Remember first the two different kinds of visual images you can make in your mind:

1. Disassociated, where YOU SEE YOURSELF IN THE PICTURE!

2. Associated, where
YOU DO NOT SEE YOURSELF IN THE PICTURE! YOU SEE THE EVENT OR CIRCUMSTANCE AS IF YOU WERE STANDING THERE, LOOKING OUT OF YOUR OWN EYES.

You'll use the first kind of image, disassociated, to imagine all the new, aggressive, powerful kinds of behaviors you'd like to have with women. That's your first step.

Your second step is to make associated images of the circumstances where you want to use those new powerful, bold, assertive behaviors. What would it actually look like from your own eyes?

Your third step is to run through the behaviors, fully associated. How would you feel in your body? What would your voice sound like? What would you be seeing out of your own eyes?

This will make these behaviors very real to your brain, and will tell your brain INSTANTLY to call them up when you need them, so you don't even have to think about it!

APPENDIX FIVE

ANCHORING TO BUILD CONFIDENCE

Step One: Recall a time when you felt very powerful, resourceful and poised.

Step Two: Close your eyes, and run through the situation. What did you see? Hear? How did it feel in your body?

Step Three: Experience those powerful feelings in your body. When they reach their peak, anchor them by reaching with your right hand and gently squeezing your left wrist, using your index finger and thumb. Keep holding that squeeze as you continue to experience those powerful feelings.

Step Four: Run through the first three steps another two times.

Step Five: Make an associated image of a circumstance where you want power and confidence with women. As you do so, fire your anchor by applying the same wrist squeeze.

Step Six: Keep holding the squeeze and you will experience the powerful, bold, confident feelings in a circumstance that used to make you nervous! You have now trained your brain to react to women by putting you into a powerful, confident, bold state, WITHOUT YOUR HAVING TO THINK ABOUT IT AT THE TIME YOU ARE ACTUALLY IN THE SITUATION!

Step Seven: Do this once a day, in the morning to start your day, for one week! Refresh and repeat after that if needed!

APPENDIX SIX

HOW TO SWIFTLY DETECT AND ELIMINATE WOMEN WHO ARE WACKOS, LOW-LIFES, CRAZIES AND SCUM

I wish the world were fair. If it were, I wouldn't be sitting here writing this. I'd be an independently wealthy multimillionaire playboy, on my own beautiful tropical island, surrounded by the entire UCLA Women's Volleyball team thinking up new ways to be nice to me.

Ahemm.

But life ISN'T fair. And one of the most unfair realities is that MOST of the women you meet are not going to be decent, intelligent, together pinnacles of love, joy and self-esteem, dying to meet you and fulfill your life in every way possible.

Nope. Most women are seriously dinged in one way or another.

Maybe it's the impossible expectations of society that does it. Maybe it's the horrible early training or just biology. Whatever the reason, it is a fact you must be prepared for.

So many times I would fall head over heels in love with a woman just because she had a few characteristics I really liked. I think I did it because I truly do like people and enjoy the feeling of liking someone.

But man, did I get my head kicked in.

Tattoo this on the inside of your eyelids: Just because a woman is gorgeous or fun or smart or (fill in your favorite here) doesn't say BEANS about her character.

Many women with great personalities have terrible characters. I've met women who are witty, brilliant and tons of fun and GORGEOUS to boot who would have no second thought about stealing you blind in a second. Or doing whatever whim crossed their mind at the moment.

These ladies live by one rule: I'M NOT GOING TO DO ANYTHING UNLESS I ABSOLUTELY FEEL LIKE IT AT THE MOMENT.

Charming flakes like this can really put your head (not to mention other parts) through the ringer.

Then there are ladies with great personalities, great characters, and even great looking. But they have one small problem:

THEY HATE SEX!

That's right. If you've ever read George Orwell's classic book, 1984, you know how the totalitarian government did it's level best to discourage people from enjoying sex. They were successful to such an extent that people viewed sex as they would a disgusting minor medical procedure like having an enema or popping a boil.

They even had a group for youngsters called THE JUNIOR ANTI-SEX LEAGUE.

Well, 1984 may have been fiction, but the JASL isn't. I've used to date many of it's members!

The best way to deal with all of these various varieties of low-life females is to take the same tact you'd take with cancer: EARLY DETECTION AND SWIFT REMOVAL.

To aid you in detection, I've designed what I call rather modestly the JEFFRIES UPRIGHT/ UPTIGHT SCALE. It allows you to quickly size up a girl to let you know if she's got relationship potential or if she deserves no more than having one of the "quick-lay" strategies pulled on her.

The vertical scale measures her enjoyment of sex. Not necessarily performance, but enthusiasm and genuine pleasure she gets out of it. Naturally, you'd want someone with a low "uptight score."

The horizontal scale measures her character, how "upright" she is. Lots of things go into this: is she warm? Does she treat people, especially strangers, with respect? DOES SHE DO WHAT SHE SAYS SHE WILL? Is she honest?

This last is most important. I once worked with a girl who I consider to be one of my models for uprightness. In addition to her regular job, which she worked with me, she sold certain door to door kitchenware/soap products. She knew I had an incredible crush on her, and would buy anything she slapped down in front of my face.

Believe me, lots and LOTS of ladies would not have hesitated to take advantage of this. But not Lisa. After talking to me for awhile, she realized that I really didn't need her products and she wouldn't let me buy them! She said she didn't feel right about making a sale to someone who could get a cheaper product that would do the same job for the particular need they had!

That, my friends, is integrity and UPRIGHTNESS.

Other qualities that go into this: Is she a giver? And, just as importantly, can SHE receive good things from YOU? Without feeling uncomfortable about it? One of the sure signs that you've got a sicko on your hands is she can't accept someone's being good to her.

Someone once described a good friend of mine this way: "She's really great to anyone who can take it."

Pick a girl who can take it.

When you meet a lady, size her up as the two of you spend time together, and try to put her on the uptight/upright scale.

Here are some early tell-tale behavioral cues to let you know you're dealing with someone who is NOT going to get a favorable spot on the scale:

1. She talks about sex on the first date. Any woman who does this either has no class, or, far more frequently, is a prickteaser. If a woman talks about sex on the first date, or even pulls out a dirty drawing or photograph to show you (believe me, I've had it happen) don't get hot and bothered! This is a sign of a sicko, believe me! Your best response is to act a trifle shocked and say, "I think talking about these kind of things with someone you hardly know is kind of vulgar, don't you?" Or, even more effective, "You know I find people who have to talk about sex right off the bat usually have a real problem with it!"

That will REALLY PUT HER IN HER PLACE. She may even try to prove you wrong, by fucking you later that night. But generally speaking, you've got a JASL member on your hands and are best off calling it an early evening. Tell her you forgot that you have to drive out of town really early the next day for a Three Stooges convention. Have some fun with it, but forget her, FAST!

2. She keeps you waiting a long time when you go to pick her up or does something else that is darn rude either at the beginning of the date or later on.

Maybe she'll pull a flaky stunt like having you wait in the living room, while she makes a quick call. Then she'll get on the phone and chat with a girlfriend for an hour or so.

Women like this are looking for a man who's going to ABUSE THEM EMOTIONALLY. They are testing you right off the bat to see if you'll be patient and understanding and if you are, YOU ARE OUT! She ideally would like you to pull the phone out of the wall, grab her by the hair and either drag her out the door or walk out, with her running after you.

If the chick pulls something like that, you have to make a decision. Either give her what she wants, by aggressively telling her what an asshole she is and turning to walk out in which case she'll fall in love with you right then and there. Or, decide she's not worth wasting the time, wave politely, and get lost. Or, wait patiently for her to finish the call and then skip the date and screw the chick right there, using a quick-lay hypnosis strategy. She certainly doesn't deserve any better treatment!

By the way, you may find it quite a mind-expanding trip to play the abusive asshole just once in your life! It is a far weirder and more mind blowing experience than any drug you might ever use — it's like being a new person, being reborn in a new personality and body. Try it, if only to see what it is like and to add to your personal flexibility.

3. She starts talking about her past boyfriends or other guys she's currently dating. This is more easily dealt with and not necessarily cause to relegate her to the "lowlife" category. Just tell her you'd really rather not hear about it. This will establish you as having some balls and then you will have passed her little test.

4. She drinks or uses drugs to excess. If she gets riotously drunk every time you go out, consider the fact that you may have an alcoholic on your hands. Sure, they can be fun for a while, but I personally would rather not be with a woman who loves Jack Daniels more than she does Ross Jeffries.

5. She does not keep appointments or commitments. I don't know how "flakes" are manufactured; I suspect that they were raised by parents who put enormous pressures on them to perform on cue, so now they have a polarity response and refuse to do anything unless they feel like it at the moment! If a woman doesn't do as she says she will, dump her or use a "quick-lay" strategy.

6. She asks for a favor BEFORE you've even gone out! Maybe she needs a ride, or some money, or even her car washed.

To hell with these evil little Nazi douche-bag exploitation queens. Fuck and dump time, good buddy! And DON'T DO HER THE FAVOR. TELL HER YOU'LL DO IT AFTER YOU GO OUT!

In summation, I'm no bible thumper, but scripture does say something very, very wise on the subject:

"A good woman, who can find her? Her price is beyond pearls."

Use the uptight/upright scale, and get yourself a STRAND OF THEM!

Free Speed Seduction Introduction Audio Tape

Send in this coupon and receive a free 60 minute audio tape from a live Speed Seduction Seminar. In addition, we will give you a free 6 month subscription to the Ross Jeffries Get Laid / Persuasion NEWSLETTER.

Name _____

Street _____

City _____

State _____ Zip Code _____

So as you think about it that way, how surprised will you be to find yourself filling out this coupon and Mailing it NOW to:

Straightforward, Inc
11918 Millpond Court
Manassas VA 20112

PS. You can also check out Ross on the net at: http://www.seduction.com

ROSS JEFFRIES

Speed Seduction Catalog

Summer 1999 $2.00

Ross's personal resource guide for power and success with women featuring his Speed Seduction(TM) technology!!!

Greetings, babe lovers! It's me again, Ross Jeffries, and once again I'm proud to be bringing you the world's best and only Speed Seduction Catalog, chocked full of <u>MY delightfully powerful</u> tapes and speed seduction home study courses guaranteed to make your love life the hottest adventure around!

These courses aren't just <u>designed</u> to pack your bed with girls; they are <u>guaranteed</u> to pack your bed with girls! That's right, <u>I personally guarantee it</u>. OK, get in there and take a look at all this great stuff; pages and pages of audio stuff, video stuff, basic stuff and advanced stuff that works. I'll be watching for your order to arrive so I can rush it out to you!

❄ ❄